Better Homes and Gardens®

75 FIX-FAST
RECIPES

Our seal assures you that every recipe in *75 Fix-Fast Recipes*
has been tested in the Better Homes and Gardens® Test Kitchen.
This means that each recipe is practical and reliable, and
meets our high standards of taste appeal.

BETTER HOMES AND GARDENS® BOOKS
Editor: Gerald M. Knox
Art Director: Ernest Shelton
Managing Editor: David A. Kirchner
Editorial Project Managers: James D. Blume, Marsha Jahns,
   Rosanne Weber Mattson, Mary Helen Schiltz

Department Head, Cook Books: Sharyl Heiken
Associate Department Heads: Sandra Granseth,
   Rosemary C. Hutchinson, Elizabeth Woolever
Senior Food Editors: Julia Malloy, Marcia Stanley, Joyce Trollope
Associate Food Editors: Linda Henry, Mary Major, Diana McMillen,
   Mary Jo Plutt, Maureen Powers, Martha Schiel,
   Linda Foley Woodrum
Test Kitchen: Director, Sharon Stilwell; Photo Studio Director,
   Janet Pittman; Home Economists: Lynn Blanchard, Jean Brekke,
   Kay Cargill, Marilyn Cornelius, Jennifer Darling,
   Maryellyn Krantz, Lynelle Munn, Dianna Nolin, Marge Steenson

Associate Art Directors: Linda Ford Vermie, Neoma Alt West,
   Randall Yontz
Assistant Art Directors: Lynda Haupert, Harijs Priekulis,
   Tom Wegner
Senior Graphic Designer: Darla Whipple-Frain
Graphic Designers: Mike Burns, Brian Wignall
Art Production: Director, John Berg; Associate, Joe Heuer;
   Office Manager, Emma Rediger

President, Book Group: Fred Stines
Vice President, General Manager: Jeramy Lanigan
Vice President, Retail Marketing: Jamie Martin
Vice President, Administrative Services: Rick Rundall

BETTER HOMES AND GARDENS® MAGAZINE
President, Magazine Group: James A. Autry
Vice President, Editorial Director: Doris Eby
Executive Director, Editorial Services: Duane L. Gregg
Food and Nutrition Editor: Nancy Byal

MEREDITH CORPORATE OFFICERS
Chairman of the Board: E. T. Meredith III
President: Robert A. Burnett
Executive Vice President: Jack D. Rehm

75 FIX-FAST RECIPES
Editor: Mary Major
Editorial Project Manager: Mary Helen Schiltz
Graphic Designer: Darla Whipple-Frain
Electronic Text Processor: Kathy Benz
Food Stylist: Janet Pittman
Contributing Photographers: Mike Dieter, Scott Little

On the front cover: Sweet and Sour Fish (page 41),
Sunshine Sauced Cake (page 65), Marinated Vegetables (page 57).

Contents

Introduction

When you're on the go from sunup to sundown, you have little time left for cooking meals. In this book we offer a simple solution. Each recipe needs only four ingredients, making for quick and easy cooking.

We've included quick-to-fix recipes for main dishes, vegetables, salads, breads, and desserts. You'll find simple recipes for both weekday meals and company dinners. Try any one of these delicious recipes and you'll be pleased with our solution to your time bind.

Ham and Broccoli Muffins

This open-face sandwich also makes a good lunch or supper dish.

1 10-ounce package
  frozen broccoli
  with cheese sauce

2 English muffins,
  split

  Dijon-style mustard

8 slices fully cooked
  ham (8 ounces)

▓ Cook broccoli with cheese sauce according to package directions. Meanwhile, toast the English muffin halves.

▓ Spread *each* English muffin half with mustard. Divide the muffin halves between 2 individual plates. Top *each* half with *two* slices of the fully cooked ham. Spoon the hot broccoli-cheese mixture over the ham. Makes 2 servings.

Shortcut Strata

Strata makes an easy weekday breakfast. Prepare the strata the night before and let it bake while you dress for work.

2 cups seasoned croutons

1 cup shredded cheddar, Swiss, *or* Monterey Jack cheese (4 ounces)

3 eggs

1½ cups light cream *or* milk

■ In an 8x1½-inch round baking dish arrange croutons in an even layer. Sprinkle cheese over croutons. In a medium mixing bowl beat eggs. Stir in cream or milk. Pour egg mixture over croutons. Cover and chill for 3 to 24 hours.

■ Bake, uncovered, in a 350° oven for 20 to 25 minutes or till a knife inserted near the center comes out clean. Let stand 5 minutes before serving. Makes 4 servings.

Making Minutes Count

When a recipe calls for chopped onion, green pepper, or nuts, save time by chopping enough for two recipes. Tightly wrap the extra in clear plastic wrap. Store onion and green pepper in the refrigerator for a few days. For longer storage, wrap in heavy-duty foil or freezer plastic wrap. Freeze onion and green pepper up to 3 months and nuts up to 6 months. You can shred extra cheese, too. Cheese keeps two weeks in the refrigerator and six months in the freezer.

Country French Toast

Canned or refrigerated eggnog makes a spicy coating.

½ cup dairy eggnog

4 thick slices French *or* Italian bread

2 tablespoons cooking oil

Powdered sugar

■ Pour eggnog into a shallow bowl. Dip both sides of French or Italian bread into eggnog.

■ In a large skillet cook bread slices in hot cooking oil over medium heat about 2½ minutes or till golden. Turn bread. Cook about 1½ minutes more or till golden. (Add more oil as needed.) Transfer to a serving plate. Sift the powdered sugar over toast. Makes 2 servings.

Ham and Potato Frittata

Traditionally a frittata cooks a few minutes under the broiler, but we found it faster and easier to just cover and let stand.

2 cups frozen hash brown potatoes with onion and peppers

3 tablespoons butter *or* margarine

6 eggs

1 cup cut-up fully cooked ham

■ In a 10-inch skillet cook hash browns in butter or margarine over medium heat till browned, stirring occasionally.

■ Meanwhile, in a medium mixing bowl beat together the eggs, 2 tablespoons *water,* and dash *pepper.* Stir in ham. Pour over potato mixture in skillet.

■ Cook over medium-low heat for 9 to 10 minutes. As eggs set, run spatula around edge of skillet, lifting edge to allow uncooked portion to flow underneath. Continue cooking and lifting edge till mixture is almost set (surface will be moist).

■ Cover skillet and remove from heat. Let stand for 3 to 4 minutes or just till top is set. Cut into wedges. Serve immediately. Makes 4 servings.

Fruit and Yogurt Breakfast

This mix-and-serve dish also tastes delicious with peaches, apples, grapes, cherries, or strawberries instead of the banana or pear.

1   **8-ounce carton fruit-flavored yogurt**

½   **cup granola**

1   **medium banana, sliced**

1   **medium pear, cored and chopped**

■ In a small mixing bowl stir together yogurt, granola, banana, and pear. Spoon into 2 serving bowls. Sprinkle each serving with additional granola, if desired. Makes 2 servings.

Push-Button Peach Shakes

Pour this drink into a paper cup for a take-it-with-you breakfast.

1 8¾-ounce can peach slices

⅓ cup nonfat dry milk powder

½ of a 6-ounce can (⅓ cup) frozen pineapple-orange *or* orange juice concentrate

4 *or* 5 ice cubes

■ In a blender container combine *undrained* peaches, milk powder, and juice concentrate. Cover and blend till smooth.

■ With the blender running, add the ice cubes, one at a time, through the opening in the lid, blending well after each addition. Garnish each serving with mint sprigs, if desired. Makes 2 (8-ounce) servings.

Beef Dill Rolls

Cubed steaks are already tenderized when you buy them. They're economical, fast-cooking, and tasty.

4 beef cubed steaks (about 1 pound total)

Dijon-style *or* **prepared mustard**

1 4- to 5-inch dill *or* **sweet pickle**

Season steaks with salt and pepper. Spread one side of each steak with mustard. Cut the pickle lengthwise into quarters. Place a pickle quarter on each steak. Roll up steaks and fasten with wooden toothpicks.

Place beef rolls on the unheated rack of a broiler pan. Broil 4 to 5 inches from heat for 6 minutes. Turn the rolls over. Broil 5 to 6 minutes more or till meat is no longer pink. Remove the toothpicks before serving. Makes 4 servings.

Salad Time-Savers

A tossed salad complements almost any hot main dish. To save yourself last-minute preparation, chop firm vegetables, such as carrots, celery, and green pepper the day before. Then wrap in plastic wrap and chill. At serving time just toss the vegetables with the salad greens and add the dressing.

Coney Island Spuds

For another meal, serve the sloppy joe topping over frankfurters in buns for traditional Coney Islands.

3 large baking potatoes

¾ pound ground beef

1 15¼-ounce can sloppy joe sauce

1 8-ounce container sour cream dip with chives

Scrub potatoes with a brush and prick skin with a fork. Bake in a 425° oven for 40 to 60 minutes or till tender.

In a skillet cook beef till brown. Drain off fat. Stir in sloppy joe sauce. Bring to boiling. Reduce heat. Cover and simmer 5 minutes. Stir in *half* the sour cream dip and ¼ cup *water*. Heat through. *Do not boil.* Quarter potatoes lengthwise. Spoon meat mixture over potatoes. Top with remaining dip. Serves 3.

Microwave Directions

Scrub potatoes and prick skin. Arrange in a spoke pattern, leaving a 1-inch space between potatoes. Micro-cook, uncovered, on 100% power (high) for 9 to 10 minutes or till slightly firm. Wrap in foil. Let stand 5 minutes. Meanwhile, crumble beef into a 1½-quart microwave-safe casserole. Micro-cook, covered, on high 3½ to 4 minutes or till brown, stirring once. Drain off fat. Stir in sloppy joe sauce. Cook, covered, on high 4 minutes or till boiling, stirring once. Cook, uncovered, on high for 2 minutes. Stir in *half* the sour cream dip and ¼ cup *water*. Cook, uncovered, on high 1 to 1½ minutes or till heated through. *Do not boil.* Continue as above.

Curly Noodle Dinner

This home-style beef-noodle dish makes a great lunch for kids.

1 pound ground beef

1 14½-ounce can stewed tomatoes

1 8-ounce can whole kernel corn

1 3-ounce package Oriental noodles with pork flavor

In a 10-inch skillet cook ground beef till brown. Drain off fat. Stir in *undrained* tomatoes, *undrained* corn, and the seasoning packet from the Oriental noodles.

Break up noodles. Stir into beef mixture. Bring to boiling. Reduce heat. Cover and simmer about 10 minutes or till the noodles are tender. Makes 4 or 5 servings.

Planning Ahead

Plan ahead to cut cooking time. Buy ingredients in the form that you'll need them for the recipe. Look for cut-up chicken, chopped nuts, bread crumbs, cracker crumbs, sliced or shredded cheese and frozen chopped onion or green pepper.

Chili Macaroni Dinner

Canned soup provides both the beans and the chili flavor.

1 cup tiny shell,
   wagon wheel, *or*
   elbow macaroni
1 pound ground beef
1 11¼-ounce can
   condensed chili
   beef soup
1 10-ounce can
   tomatoes with
   green chili
   peppers

Cook macaroni according to package directions. Drain. Rinse with cold water. Drain again. Set aside.

In a medium skillet cook ground beef till brown. Drain off fat. Stir in macaroni, soup, and *undrained* tomatoes with chili peppers. Cook till heated through. Makes 4 servings.

Microwave Directions

Cook macaroni as directed above.

Crumble beef in a 2-quart nonmetal casserole. Micro-cook, covered, on 100% power (high) for 4 to 5 minutes or till no pink remains, stirring once. Drain off fat. Stir in macaroni, soup, and *undrained* tomatoes with chili peppers. Cook, covered, on high for 5 to 7 minutes or till hot, stirring once.

Speedy Beef Stroganoff

8 ounces sliced
   cooked beef

1 12-ounce jar
   mushroom gravy

1 8-ounce container
   sour cream dip
   with toasted
   onion

Hot cooked noodles

Cut beef into juliennne strips. In a medium saucepan combine the beef strips and mushroom gravy. Cook over medium heat till mixture is hot and bubbly, stirring occasionally.

Stir some of the hot mixture into sour cream dip. Return sour cream mixture to meat mixture. Cook over low heat till heated through. Serve over noodles. Makes 3 servings.

Microwave Directions

Cut beef into julienne strips. In a 1½-quart nonmetal casserole combine beef strips and mushroom gravy. Micro-cook, covered, on 100% power (high) for 4 to 5 minutes or till mixture is hot, stirring once.

Stir some of the hot mixture into the sour cream dip. Return sour cream mixture to meat mixture. Cook, covered, for 2 to 3 minutes. Serve over noodles.

Steak with Mustard Sauce

The sauce also complements broiled pork chops or chicken.

1 pound beef sirloin steak, cut 1 inch thick

3 tablespoons mayonnaise *or* salad dressing

2 tablespoons Dijon-style mustard

1 tablespoon lemon juice

Slash the fat edge of steak at 1-inch intervals without cutting into the meat. Place steak on an unheated rack in a broiler pan. Broil steak 3 to 4 inches from heat for 7 minutes.

Meanwhile, for sauce, in small bowl stir together mayonnaise or salad dressing, mustard, and lemon juice. Set aside.

Season steak with salt and pepper. Turn meat using tongs. Broil 6 to 8 minutes more for medium doneness. Season again with salt and pepper. Brush with some of the sauce. Broil 1 to 2 minutes more. To serve, thinly slice steak. Pass the remaining sauce. Makes 4 servings.

Attention Microwave Owners

Recipes with microwave directions were tested in countertop microwave ovens that operate on 600 to 700 watts. Cooking times are approximate since microwave ovens vary by manufacturer.

Beef Teriyaki

Spoon this saucy beef-and-vegetable combo over rice.

1 **pound beef top round steak**

1 **tablespoon cooking oil**

3 **cups loose-pack frozen broccoli, French-style green beans, onions, and red peppers**

⅓ **cup teriyaki sauce**

Partially freeze beef. Cut on bias into thin strips.

Preheat wok or large skillet over high heat. Add cooking oil. (Add more oil as necessary.) Stir-fry frozen vegetables for 3 to 4 minutes or till crisp-tender. Remove vegetables from wok.

Add *half* of the beef to the hot oil. Stir-fry for 2 to 3 minutes or till done. Remove cooked beef. Repeat with remaining beef. Return all the beef to the wok. Stir in teriyaki sauce and vegetables. Cook till heated through. Makes 4 servings.

Microwave Directions

Slice beef as directed above. Preheat 10-inch microwave browning dish on 100% power (high) for 5 minutes. Add oil and beef. Micro-cook, uncovered, on high for 2 to 4 minutes or till no longer pink, stirring once. Remove beef. Drain. Cook vegetables and 2 tablespoons *water* in browning dish, covered, on high 4 to 6 minutes or till crisp-tender. Drain. Stir in beef and sauce. Cook, covered, on high 1 to 2 minutes or till hot.

Fast Fajitas

These easy-to-make fajitas (pronounced fah-HEE-tahs) use a package of frozen sliced beef.

8 6-inch flour tortillas

1 14-ounce package frozen thinly sliced beef

½ cup sour cream dip with chives

½ cup salsa

Wrap tortillas in foil. Warm in a 350° oven for 5 minutes. Meanwhile, prepare beef according to package directions. Cut beef into bite-size strips.

For each fajita, arrange *one-eighth* of the beef strips on top of *each* tortilla to within 1 inch of edge. Spoon *1 tablespoon* sour cream dip and *1 tablespoon* salsa onto *each* tortilla. Roll up each tortilla. Makes 4 servings.

Bavarian Beef Sandwiches

Sweet-sour cabbage adds tang to this roast beef sandwich.

8 slices dark rye bread

8 ounces thinly sliced, cooked beef

8 teaspoons Thousand Island salad dressing

1 16-ounce jar sweet-sour cabbage, drained

On *each* of *four* slices dark rye bread layer *2 ounces* sliced cooked beef. Drizzle *2 teaspoons* salad dressing over *each*. Spoon *one-fourth* of the sweet-sour cabbage over *each*. Top *each* with a slice of dark rye bread. Makes 4 servings.

Buying Beef

When you need cooked beef for a recipe, buy roast beef from your deli. Have it sliced thinly for *Bavarian Beef Sandwiches*, but for cooked dishes, such as *Speedy Beef Stroganoff* (see recipe, page 15), have it sliced about ⅛ inch thick.

Ham-It-Up Sauce

Try this maple-syrup-and-mustard sauce on chicken, too.

2 tablespoons maple-flavored syrup *or* maple syrup

2 tablespoons brown mustard

1 6-ounce package sliced fully cooked ham

For glaze, in a small saucepan stir together maple-flavored syrup or maple syrup and brown mustard. Cook till heated through. Arrange ham on dinner plates. Spoon the warm glaze over ham. Makes 2 servings.

Microwave Directions

In a 1-cup glass measure combine syrup and mustard. Micro-cook, uncovered, on 100% power (high) for 30 to 45 seconds or till heated through, stirring once. Arrange ham on 2 dinner plates. Spoon the warm glaze over the ham.

Chili-Frank Burritos

We took all-American hot dogs and wrapped them in tortillas for a south-of-the-border flavor.

2 7-inch flour tortillas

2 slices American cheese *or* cheese spread

2 chili-stuffed frankfurters

▨ Wrap tortillas in foil. Heat in a 375° oven 5 minutes.

▨ On top of each tortilla arrange *one* slice cheese or cheese spread and *one* frankfurter. Fold in ends of tortillas. Roll up tortillas around cheese and frankfurters. Wrap in foil. Bake in the 375° oven about 15 minutes or till warm. Makes 2 servings.

The Well-Stocked Kitchen

Convenience foods are the busy cook's best friend. Keep a supply of canned or frozen meats, poultry, fish, or seafood; canned or frozen fruits or vegetables; pasta or rice mixes; and cheese for days when you don't have time to cook. Turn to the index and find the category for the food you have, such as chicken. Then select one of the recipes. In no time at all, you'll be able to put a meal on the table.

Italian Sausage Dinner

For a different taste, substitute fresh Polish sausage or knackwurst for the Italian sausage.

1 1-pound fresh Italian sausage link

1 small onion, thinly sliced and separated into rings

2 cups sliced fresh mushrooms

1 green pepper, cut into 1-inch pieces

In a medium skillet place sausage, onion, and ½ cup *water*. Cover and cook over medium-low heat for 15 minutes. Drain.

Add mushrooms and green pepper. Cover and cook for 5 to 10 minutes more or till sausage is browned and vegetables are crisp-tender. Makes 3 servings.

Quick Ham Jambalaya

For a different flavor, try chicken or shrimp in place of the ham.

2 cups cubed fully cooked ham *or* two 6¾-ounce cans chunk-style ham, broken up

1 10-ounce can tomatoes with green chili peppers

1 cup quick-cooking rice

1 teaspoon chili powder

In a medium skillet combine ham, *undrained* tomatoes with green chili peppers, *uncooked* rice, chili powder, and ½ cup *water*. Cook over high heat till mixture boils. Reduce heat to low. Cover and cook about 8 minutes or till all the liquid is absorbed. Makes 4 servings.

Shopping List Know-How

A little organization beforehand pays off by saving you time in the grocery store. Begin by writing down food categories, such as dairy products, fruits and vegetables, meats, frozen foods, baked goods, staples, and nonfood items. Think about the layout of the store where you shop and organize the categories according to the store's floor plan. Then list the items you need under each category.

Creamed Ham With Peas

Use either homemade or purchased corn bread or biscuits.

1 **10-ounce package frozen peas in cream sauce**

1 **cup cut-up fully cooked ham**

½ **cup shredded American cheese (2 ounces)**

Corn bread *or* biscuits

■ In a medium saucepan cook frozen peas in cream sauce according to package directions.

■ Stir ham and cheese into peas and sauce in the saucepan. Cook over low heat till heated through and cheese is melted, stirring occasionally. To serve, spoon the ham mixture over corn bread or biscuits. Makes 3 servings.

Microwave Directions

■ In a 1-quart nonmetal casserole micro-cook peas in cream sauce according to package directions.

■ Stir ham and cheese into peas and sauce in the casserole. Cover and micro-cook on 100% power (high) for 2 to 3 minutes or till heated through and cheese is melted, stirring once. Serve as directed above.

Brats and Onions

For a taste of Bavaria, serve with pumpernickel bread.

4 cups sliced onions

2 tablespoons butter *or* margarine

2 tablespoons brown mustard

8 fully cooked bratwurst *or* smoked sausage links (1 pound total)

In a large saucepan combine sliced onions and butter or margarine. Cover and cook over medium heat about 5 minutes or till onions are almost tender, stirring occasionally. Stir mustard into the onion mixture.

Meanwhile, score the bratwurst or smoked sausage links ¼ inch deep at 1-inch intervals. Add the sausage. Cook, covered, for 10 to 12 minutes more or till the onions are tender and the sausage is heated through. Makes 4 servings.

Microwave Directions

Place sliced onions and butter or margarine in a 2-quart microwave-safe casserole. Micro-cook, covered, on 100% power (high) about 8 minutes or till the onions are almost tender, stirring once. Stir mustard into onion mixture.

Meanwhile, score sausages as directed above. Add to onion mixture. Cook, covered, on high 6 to 8 minutes or till onions are tender and sausage is hot, giving dish a half-turn once.

Salami Reubens

To make an already spunky sandwich even spunkier, drizzle Italian salad dressing over salami after baking.

8 **4-** *or* **5-inch slices salami**

4 **slices Swiss** *or* **caraway cheese**

1 **cup sauerkraut, rinsed and drained**

4 **frankfurter buns, split**

On a flat surface arrange *two* slices salami so edges overlap. Repeat 3 times, using all the salami. Top *each* pair with *one* slice of cheese and ¼ *cup* sauerkraut. Fold edges of salami over cheese and sauerkraut. Place *each* bundle in a frankfurter bun. Wrap *each* bun in foil. Place on a baking sheet.

Bake in a 375° oven about 15 minutes or till the cheese is melted. Makes 4 servings.

Microwave Directions

On a flat surface arrange *two* slices salami so edges overlap. Repeat 3 times, using all the salami. Top *each* pair with *one* slice of cheese and ¼ *cup* sauerkraut. Fold edges of salami over cheese and sauerkraut. Place *each* bundle in a frankfurter bun. Wrap *each* bun in a microwave-safe paper towel.

Arrange buns in a microwave oven. Micro-cook on 100% power (high) about 2 minutes or till cheese is melted.

Doubleheader Pizza

Two pizzas are better than one—especially when they're served as a sandwich, like these frozen pizzas.

2 13-ounce frozen cheese pizzas

1 8-ounce package brown-and-serve sausage links

¼ cup sliced pimiento-stuffed olives

1 4-ounce package shredded mozzarella cheese

Place *one* cheese pizza on a greased baking sheet. Cut sausage links into ¼-inch-thick slices. Arrange sausage slices and olives on top. Sprinkle with *half* of the cheese. Top with remaining cheese pizza, crust side up.

Cover the entire pizza with foil. Bake in a 375° oven for 30 minutes. Uncover and bake for 10 minutes more.

Sprinkle the remaining mozzarella cheese over pizza. Bake 5 minutes more or till cheese is melted. Makes 6 servings.

Sesame Pork Chops

Bottled barbecue sauce and apricot preserves make an easy sauce for these broiled chops.

¼ **cup bottled barbecue sauce**

2 **tablespoons apricot preserves**

1 **tablespoon sesame seed, toasted**

4 **pork loin chops, cut ¾ inch thick (1½ to 1¾ pounds total)**

For sauce, in a small saucepan stir together barbecue sauce and apricot preserves. Cook over low heat just till preserves melt. Stir in sesame seed. Remove from heat.

Trim fat from chops. Season with salt and pepper. Place chops on an unheated rack in a broiler pan. Broil 3 to 4 inches from the heat for 10 minutes. Brush chops with sauce. Turn chops over. Broil 10 to 15 minutes more or till no longer pink, brushing with sauce during last 5 minutes. Makes 4 servings.

Salami Couscous Salad

Line the serving bowl or individual plates with lettuce leaves.

½ of a 9-ounce
    package frozen
    cut green beans

⅔ cup ready-to-cook
    couscous

8 ounces sliced
    salami

½ cup Italian salad
    dressing

Cook green beans according to package directions. Drain. Rinse with cold water. Drain again.

Meanwhile, place couscous in a large mixing bowl. Pour ⅔ cup boiling *water* over couscous. Let stand 5 minutes.

Cut the salami slices into wedges. Stir salami, cooked beans, and Italian salad dressing into couscous. Mix well. Cover and chill for 2 to 3 hours or till serving time. Makes 3 servings.

Pronto Chicken And Grapes

To save even more time, purchase boneless, halved chicken breasts.

2 whole medium chicken breasts (about 1½ pounds total)

¼ cup sweet Marsala *or* cream sherry

2 tablespoons butter *or* margarine

½ cup seedless red *or* green grapes, halved

Skin and bone chicken breasts. Cut in half lengthwise. Place the chicken breast halves in a shallow dish. Pour Marsala or sherry over chicken. Marinate for 20 to 30 minutes at room temperature, turning chicken once or twice. Drain chicken, reserving marinade. Pat chicken dry with paper towels. Sprinkle chicken lightly with salt and pepper.

In a large skillet melt butter or margarine. Add chicken. Cook over medium-high heat about 4 minutes on each side or till chicken is brown and tender. Transfer chicken to serving plates. Cover to keep warm.

For sauce, add reserved marinade and grapes to skillet. Cook and stir till mixture boils. Boil, uncovered, about 30 seconds to reduce slightly. Pour over chicken. Makes 4 servings.

Shanghai Skillet

If you'd like, cook another package of pea pods and arrange them around the meat-and-rice mixture.

1 6-ounce package frozen pea pods

1 8-ounce package turkey ham luncheon meat

1 6¼-ounce package regular stir-fried rice mix

■ Place pea pods in a colander and rinse under running water to thaw and separate. Cut pea pods in half crosswise. Cut turkey ham luncheon meat into julienne strips.

■ In a 2-quart saucepan prepare rice mix according to package directions. Stir in pea pods and *three-fourths* of the turkey ham. Cover and let stand for 5 minutes. Turn into a serving dish. Top with remaining turkey ham. Makes 4 servings.

Spice It Up

Seasoning blends save you time because you sprinkle only one seasoning instead of several. When you want a little extra flavor, try sprinkling fines herbes or Italian seasoning over broiled steaks, hamburgers, chicken, or fish. Add a little lemon pepper to a fish or chicken dish. For desserts, sprinkle pumpkin-pie or apple-pie spice over puddings or ice cream.

Clock-Watcher Cacciatore

Cacciatore means cooked with tomatoes and herbs. This version gets both from the convenient chunky-style spaghetti sauce.

8 chicken drumsticks *or* thighs (about 2 pounds)

1 15½-ounce jar chunky meatless spaghetti sauce

1 green pepper, cut into ½-inch-wide strips

Grated Parmesan cheese

In a medium nonstick skillet place chicken drumsticks or thighs, skin side down. Cook over medium heat about 15 minutes or till browned, turning frequently. Drain off fat.

Add spaghetti sauce and green pepper to skillet. Cover and cook over low heat for 30 to 35 minutes or till chicken is tender. Transfer chicken to a serving platter. Stir mixture in skillet. Pour over chicken. Pass the Parmesan cheese to sprinkle atop. Makes 4 servings.

Microwave Directions

Arrange the chicken in a 12x7½x2-inch microwave-safe baking dish with meatiest portions toward the outside of dish. Add the green pepper. Cover dish with waxed paper. Micro-cook on 100% power (high) for 10 minutes, giving the dish a half-turn once. Drain off fat. Rearrange the chicken pieces.

Spoon the sauce over chicken. Cook, covered, on high about 8 minutes more or till the chicken is tender. Serve as above.

Curry-Up Chow Mein

For an easy, Indian-style garnish and extra flavor, top each serving with chopped unsalted peanuts.

1   15¼-ounce can
    chicken stew

1   medium apple,
    cored and
    chopped

1   teaspoon curry
    powder

    Chow mein noodles

In a medium saucepan stir together chicken stew, apple, and curry powder. Cook over medium heat for 8 to 10 minutes or till heated through, stirring occasionally. Serve over chow mein noodles. Makes 2 servings.

Microwave Directions

In a 1-quart microwave-safe casserole stir together chicken stew, apple, and curry powder. Micro-cook, covered, on 100% power (high) for 4 to 5 minutes or till heated through, stirring once. Serve over chow mein noodles.

Scotch Eggs

These sausage-wrapped eggs make great snacks, too.

10 eggs

1 pound ground turkey sausage

⅔ cup crushed rich round crackers (about 16 crackers)

Chili sauce (optional)

To hard-cook eggs, place *eight* of the eggs in shells in a large saucepan. Add enough water to cover eggs. Bring to a rapid boil over high heat. Reduce heat so water is just below simmering. Cover and cook for 15 to 20 minutes. Pour off water. Run cold water over eggs.

Divide turkey sausage into 8 portions. Shape each portion into a 4-inch-round patty. Wrap *each* patty around *one* hard-cooked egg, covering egg completely.

In a small bowl beat the remaining eggs. Roll each sausage-wrapped egg in the beaten eggs, then roll in crushed crackers.

Arrange eggs in a shallow baking pan. Bake in a 375° oven for 25 to 30 minutes or till sausage is no longer pink. Serve warm or cold with chili sauce, if desired. Makes 8 servings.

Chicken with Biscuits

For extra bite, use Monterey Jack cheese with jalapeño peppers.

1 19-ounce can chunky chicken vegetable soup

1 cup chopped cooked chicken *or* **one 5-ounce can chunk-style chicken**

1 cup shredded Monterey Jack cheese (4 ounces)

Biscuits

In a medium saucepan combine soup, chicken, and cheese. Cook over medium heat till cheese melts and mixture is hot, stirring occasionally.

To serve, spoon chicken mixture into 3 individual bowls. Top with biscuits. Makes 3 servings.

Microwave Directions

In a 1½-quart nonmetal casserole combine soup, chicken, and cheese. Cover and micro-cook on 100% power (high) for 4 to 6 minutes or till mixture is hot and bubbly, stirring once.

Serve as directed above.

Orange-Chicken Kabobs

Stir some snipped parsley into hot cooked rice and serve with these sweet and tangy kabobs.

2 whole medium chicken breasts (about 1½ pounds total)

1 large green *or* sweet red pepper, cut into 1½-inch pieces

½ cup orange marmalade

2 tablespoons vinegar

Skin and bone chicken breasts. Cut in half lengthwise. Cut each chicken breast half into 4 lengthwise strips. To thread kabobs, skewer one end of a chicken strip. Next, thread a green or red pepper piece. Then thread another portion of chicken. Repeat threading of chicken and pepper, adding chicken strips as needed, to fill 4 skewers.

For glaze, stir together orange marmalade and vinegar.

Place kabobs in a single layer on an unheated rack in a broiler pan. Broil kabobs 4 to 5 inches from heat for 6 minutes. Brush kabobs with glaze. Turn kabobs. Broil 6 to 8 minutes more or till the chicken is tender, brushing once or twice with glaze. Makes 4 servings.

Lemon-Rosemary Chicken

Garnish each plate with a lemon slice and fresh rosemary.

⅓ cup lemon juice

¼ cup cooking oil

1½ teaspoons snipped fresh rosemary *or* ½ teaspoon dried rosemary, crushed

2 whole medium chicken breasts (about 1½ pounds total)

■ For marinade, combine lemon juice, oil, fresh or dried rosemary, ¼ teaspoon *salt*, and ⅛ teaspoon *pepper*.

■ Skin and bone chicken breasts. Cut in half lengthwise. Place chicken in a plastic bag. Place bag in a bowl. Pour the marinade over chicken. Close bag and marinate in the refrigerator for 6 hours or overnight.

■ Remove chicken from marinade, reserving marinade. Place chicken on an unheated rack in a broiler pan. Broil 4 to 5 inches from heat for 6 minutes. Turn chicken. Brush with marinade. Broil 6 to 8 minutes more or till chicken is tender, brushing once or twice with marinade. Serves 6.

Chicken Salad In Melon Boats

Creamy coleslaw provides the dressing for this fruity chicken salad.

1 pint deli creamy coleslaw

2 5½-ounce cans chunk-style chicken, drained and broken up

½ cup halved strawberries *or* seedless grapes

1 medium cantaloupe

In a medium mixing bowl combine coleslaw, chicken, and strawberries or grapes. Toss gently to mix. Cover and chill in the freezer for 15 minutes.

Meanwhile, cut cantaloupe lengthwise into 4 wedges. Discard seeds. Fill *each* cantaloupe wedge with *one-fourth* of the chicken mixture. Makes 4 servings.

Meal Planning

A little bit of planning is well worth the time. Plan meals for several days at once. Team a main dish that requires some preparation with a ready-made dessert, or vice versa. Then make out a complete grocery list of all the items you need.

Peppered Turkey Salad

Stir-fry the turkey strips and then let them marinate in an oil-and-vinegar salad dressing.

2 boneless turkey breast tenderloin steaks (8 ounces total)

½ cup oil-and-vinegar salad dressing

2 red, green, *or* yellow sweet peppers

2 cups torn lettuce

Cut tenderloin steaks into ½-inch-wide strips. In a 10-inch skillet heat *¼ cup* oil-and-vinegar salad dressing. Add turkey strips. Stir-fry over medium-high heat for 3 to 4 minutes or till tender. Remove from heat. Cool slightly.

Cut peppers into strips. In a medium mixing bowl combine peppers and *undrained* turkey. Pour the remaining oil-and-vinegar salad dressing over turkey mixture. Toss to coat. Cover and chill several hours or overnight. To serve, arrange lettuce on 2 dinner plates. Drain the turkey mixture. Spoon over lettuce. Makes 2 servings.

Chicken-Vegetable Chowder

Put away your knife. You make this soup with products that come already sliced or chopped.

1 5¼- or 5¾-ounce package dry au gratin potato mix *or* other dry scalloped potato mix

3 cups milk

2 cups loose-pack frozen mixed zucchini, carrot, cauliflower, lima beans, and Italian beans

8 ounces (1½ cups) frozen chopped cooked chicken *or* two 5-ounce cans chunk-style chicken

In a 3-quart saucepan combine potatoes from the mix and 4 cups *water*. Bring to boiling. Reduce heat. Cook, covered, about 15 minutes or till potatoes are nearly tender. Drain.

Stir sauce mix from potato mix, milk, vegetables, and chicken into the potato mixture in saucepan. Bring to boiling. Reduce heat. Cook 5 to 8 minutes or till vegetables are crisp-tender and mixture is slightly thickened. Makes 4 or 5 servings.

Sweet and Sour Fish

Keep the ingredients on hand for this frozen fish fix-up. (Pictured on the cover.)

1 **14-ounce package frozen breaded fish fillets**

1 **9-ounce jar sweet and sour sauce**

1 **8¼-ounce can pineapple chunks, drained**

½ **of a medium sweet red *or* green pepper, cut into strips**

Cook fish fillets according to package directions.

Meanwhile, in a small saucepan combine sweet and sour sauce, pineapple, and red or green pepper. Cover and cook over low heat about 5 minutes or till the pepper is tender. Serve sauce with fish fillets. Makes 3 or 4 servings.

Asparagus-Fish Rolls

Prepare a package of long-grain-and-wild-rice mix to serve with this elegant fish dish.

4 3-ounce fresh *or* frozen fish fillets (about ¼ inch thick)

1 10-ounce package frozen asparagus spears

2 tablespoons butter *or* margarine, melted

Lemon pepper

Thaw fish, if frozen. Cook asparagus according to package directions. Place 4 to 6 asparagus spears across the boned side of each fillet. Roll up, jelly-roll style, starting from narrow end. Secure with wooden toothpicks, if necessary. Place rolls, seam side down, in a 10x6x2-inch baking dish. Brush with butter or margarine. Sprinkle with lemon pepper and salt.

Bake in a 375° oven for 18 to 20 minutes or till fish flakes easily with a fork. Remove toothpicks. Makes 4 servings.

Microwave Directions

Assemble the fish rolls as directed above. Place rolls, seam side down, in a nonmetal 10x6x2-inch baking dish. Brush rolls with melted butter. Sprinkle with lemon pepper and salt. Cover dish with vented microwave-safe plastic wrap.

Micro-cook on 100% power (high) for 2 minutes. Carefully rearrange rolls. Cook, covered, on high for 2 to 4 minutes more or till fish flakes easily with a fork. Remove toothpicks.

Mexican Crumb Fish

For a Mexican touch, serve with shredded lettuce and chili peppers.

1 11½- to 12-ounce
  package frozen
  fish portions

1 tablespoon butter *or*
  margarine, melted

1 teaspoon chili
  powder

¼ cup coarsely
  crushed rich
  round crackers

In a shallow baking dish arrange the frozen fish portions in a single layer. Combine melted butter or margarine and chili powder. Drizzle over fillets.

Bake in a 500° oven for 11 to 12 minutes or till fish flakes easily when tested with a fork. Sprinkle cracker crumbs over fish. Bake 1 minute more. Makes 4 servings.

Fish Bits

Fish fits right in with today's busy life-styles. It cooks quickly and lends itself to lots of flavor combinations. In addition, it's rich in protein, vitamins, and minerals, yet low in calories and fat.

Frozen fish is readily available in most grocery stores. When buying frozen fish, look for packages without holes or tears. Also, for the best product, look for frost-free packages.

Tomato-Topped Fish

The bacon, onion, and tomato topping tastes good with frozen breaded fish fillets, too.

1 pound fresh *or* frozen fish fillets

6 slices bacon

1 medium onion, sliced

1 medium tomato, chopped

Thaw fish, if frozen.

In a large skillet cook bacon over medium-low heat for 6 to 8 minutes or till crisp, turning often. Remove bacon and drain on paper towels. Add onion to drippings in skillet. Cook 5 to 7 minutes or till tender. Drain. Stir in tomato. Bring to boiling. Reduce heat. Cover and simmer 1 to 2 minutes or till heated through. Crumble bacon and stir into tomato mixture.

Meanwhile, measure thickness of fish fillets. Place in a shallow baking dish, tucking under any thin edges. Sprinkle lightly with salt and pepper. Cover with foil. Bake in a 450° oven till fish flakes easily when tested with a fork (allow 5 to 7 minutes per ½-inch thickness of fish). To serve, spoon tomato mixture over fish fillets. Makes 4 servings.

Seafood Shells

A tortilla shell holds this creamy mock-crab and vegetable filling.

3 6-inch flour tortillas

1 10-ounce package frozen mixed Mexican-style vegetables

1 10¾-ounce can chunky creamy mushroom soup

1 8-ounce package frozen salad-style crab-flavored fish, thawed

For tortilla shells, wrap flour tortillas in foil and heat in a 350° oven for 10 minutes. Fit each tortilla into a greased 10-ounce custard cup. Place on a baking sheet. Bake in the 350° oven for 12 to 15 minutes or till light brown. Transfer tortilla shells from custard cups to 3 serving plates.

Meanwhile, cook frozen vegetables according to package directions. Stir in mushroom soup. Gently stir fish into vegetable mixture. Heat through. Spoon the fish mixture into the tortilla shells. Makes 3 servings.

Pasta with Clam Sauce

Start cooking the pasta first, because it takes longer to cook.

6 ounces spinach, tomato, *and/or* plain corkscrew macaroni *or* linguine

1 10¾-ounce can condensed New England clam chowder

1 6½-ounce can minced clams, drained

3 tablespoons dry white wine

Cook the pasta according to package directions. Drain.

Meanwhile, in a medium saucepan combine clam chowder and minced clams. Cook over medium heat till hot and bubbly, stirring occasionally. Stir in wine. Toss hot clam mixture with pasta. Makes 3 servings.

Microwave Directions

Cook pasta according to package directions. Drain.

In 1-quart nonmetal casserole combine chowder and clams. Cover and micro-cook on 100% power (high) for 3½ to 4½ minutes or till hot. Stir in wine. Toss with pasta.

Poached Fish with Horseradish Sauce

The sour-cream sauce tastes delicious over any cooked fish.

1 pound fresh *or*
    frozen salmon *or*
    halibut steaks,
    cut ¾ to 1 inch
    thick

½ cup sour cream dip
    with chives

1 to 2 teaspoons
    prepared
    horseradish

Thaw fish, if frozen. In a large skillet bring 2 cups lightly salted *water* just to boiling. Measure the thickness of fish steaks. Carefully add the fish. Return just to boiling, then reduce heat. Cover and simmer gently till the fish flakes easily when tested with a fork (allow 4 to 6 minutes per ½-inch thickness of fish). Drain.

Meanwhile, for sauce, stir together sour cream dip and horseradish. Serve sauce over fish. Garnish with parsley and a radish rose, if desired. Makes 4 servings.

2-Minute Tuna-Mac Salad

1 pint deli macaroni salad

1 3¼-ounce can tuna, drained and flaked

½ cup sliced radishes

Lettuce leaves

In a medium mixing bowl combine macaroni salad, tuna, and radishes. Toss gently to mix. Cover and chill till serving time. Serve on 2 lettuce-lined plates. Makes 2 servings.

The Big Chill

Store canned fruit, chicken, tuna, and other foods that you plan to serve cold in the refrigerator. You'll reduce the chilling time needed for your salad or cold dish. If refrigerator space is at a premium, chill the cans in the freezer for up to 20 minutes (don't leave them in any longer or the cans may burst).

Creamy Broccoli And Noodles

Mixed vegetables, cauliflower, or carrots make tasty substitutes for the broccoli in this creamy sauce and pasta.

1 10-ounce package frozen cut broccoli

½ cup milk

1 3-ounce package cream cheese with chives, cubed

5 ounces mafalda noodles (curly-edge wide noodles) *or* **linguine**

■ For the sauce, in a medium saucepan cook broccoli according to package directions. Drain. Remove broccoli and set aside.

■ In the same saucepan combine the milk and the cream cheese with chives. Heat and stir till smooth. Stir in the broccoli. Season to taste with salt and pepper.

■ Meanwhile, cook the mafalda or linguine according to package directions. Drain. Arrange the pasta on 3 serving plates. Pour the broccoli sauce over pasta. Makes 3 servings.

Crowning Glory Vegetables

Use this elegant soufflélike topper to jazz up any combination of frozen vegetables.

1 16-ounce package loose-pack frozen mixed carrots, cauliflower, green beans, zucchini, and butter beans (5 cups)

3 egg whites

½ cup mayonnaise *or* salad dressing

¼ cup shredded cheddar cheese (1 ounce)

■ In a medium saucepan cook mixed vegetables according to the package directions. Drain well. Divide vegetables among four 10-ounce custard cups.

■ In a small mixer bowl beat egg whites and *¼ teaspoon* salt with an electric mixer on medium speed till stiff peaks form (tips stand straight). Fold in mayonnaise or salad dressing.

■ Spoon mayonnaise mixture atop vegetables in custard cups. Sprinkle with cheddar cheese. Bake, uncovered, in a 350° oven for 12 to 15 minutes or till egg-white mixture is golden and vegetables are heated through. Makes 4 servings.

Cauliflower Chowder

For variety, use one can of each soup.

1 **10-ounce package frozen cauliflower**

2 **10¾-ounce cans condensed cream of potato soup** *or* **two 11¼-ounce cans condensed green pea soup**

2 **cups milk**

1 **cup shredded Swiss cheese (4 ounces)**

▢ In a large saucepan combine cauliflower and *½ cup* water. Cover and cook about 5 minutes or till tender. *Do not drain.* Cut up large pieces. Mash all of the cauliflower slightly.

▢ Stir in the condensed potato soup or green pea soup. Stir in milk and Swiss cheese. Cook and stir till cheese is melted and soup is heated through. Makes 6 servings.

Microwave Directions

▢ In a 3-quart microwave-safe casserole combine cauliflower and *½ cup* water. Micro-cook, covered, on 100% power (high) for 6 to 8 minutes or till cauliflower is tender. *Do not drain.* Cut up large pieces. Mash cauliflower slightly.

▢ Stir in condensed potato soup or pea soup. Stir in milk and cheese. Cook, covered, on high for 8 to 10 minutes or till cheese is melted and soup is heated through, stirring twice.

Herbed Potatoes

Choose either basil, oregano, or tarragon to season these potatoes.

3 medium potatoes

1 medium onion

½ teaspoon dried basil,
   oregano, *or*
   tarragon, crushed

2 tablespoons butter
   or margarine,
   melted

■ Thinly slice potatoes and onion. In a 9-inch pie plate layer *half* of the potatoes and *half* of the onion. Sprinkle with *half* of the herb. Drizzle with *half* of the butter or margarine. Repeat the potato, onion, herb, and butter or margarine layers. Season with salt and pepper.

■ Cover with foil and bake in a 425° oven for 20 minutes. Uncover and bake for 10 to 20 minutes more or till the potatoes are tender. Makes 4 servings.

Apple-of-Your-Eye Rice

Try this fruited rice with a pork chop or chicken dinner.

1 **10-ounce package frozen long grain and wild rice**

1 **medium apple, cored and coarsely chopped**

¼ **cup raisins *or* chopped pecans**

■ Place the rice pouch in a medium mixing bowl filled with hot *water*. Let stand about 10 minutes or till rice is just thawed. Remove the pouch from water.

■ Remove rice from the pouch and place in a medium saucepan. Stir in apple, raisins or pecans, and *2 tablespoons* water. Cover and cook about 5 minutes or till rice is heated through and apple is crisp-tender, stirring occasionally. Makes 4 servings.

Spanish Rice Peppers

Pepper halves make tasty servers for this savory rice.

2 medium green *or* red sweet peppers

½ cup long grain rice

⅓ cup chili sauce

¾ cup shredded sharp American cheese (3 ounces)

Cut peppers in half lengthwise. Remove membrane and seeds. Chop *one* pepper half. Set aside. Cook the remaining *three* pepper halves in boiling salted water for 5 minutes. Drain.

Meanwhile, in a small saucepan cook rice according to package directions, *except* add the chopped pepper.

Stir chili sauce and *¼ cup* of the shredded cheese into the cooked rice. Divide the mixture among the 3 pepper halves.

Place the filled pepper halves in an 8x8x2-inch baking dish. Cover dish with foil. Bake in a 350° oven for 15 to 20 minutes or till the rice mixture is heated through.

Sprinkle peppers with remaining cheese. Bake for 2 to 3 minutes more or till the cheese is melted. Makes 3 servings.

Mexaroni and Cheese

Add an extra kick to this macaroni dish with several dashes of bottled hot pepper sauce.

1 10-ounce can tomatoes with green chili peppers

1 small green pepper, coarsely chopped

1 14¾-ounce can macaroni and cheese

In a medium skillet combine *undrained* tomatoes with green chili peppers and green pepper. Cook, covered, over medium heat about 5 minutes or till green pepper is crisp-tender.

Stir in macaroni and cheese. Cook over medium heat for 3 to 5 minutes or till the mixture is heated through, stirring occasionally. Makes 4 servings.

Microwave Directions

In a 1-quart microwave-safe casserole combine *undrained* tomatoes with green chili peppers and chopped green pepper. Micro-cook, covered, on 100% power (high) for 2 to 3 minutes or till green pepper is crisp-tender.

Stir in macaroni and cheese. Cook, covered, on high for 3 to 5 minutes or till heated through, stirring once.

Fruit and Spinach Salad

Here's a slick trick for washing spinach: Place it in a bowl of lukewarm water for a few minutes, swirl, then lift from water.

1 **17-ounce can fruit cocktail**

4 **cups torn spinach**

¼ **cup raisins**

¼ **cup mayonnaise *or* salad dressing**

Drain fruit cocktail, reserving *1 tablespoon* of the liquid. In a large mixing bowl combine fruit cocktail, torn spinach, and raisins. Toss gently to mix.

For dressing, combine reserved liquid and mayonnaise or salad dressing. Cover and chill spinach mixture and dressing separately for at least 1 hour. Before serving, add dressing to the spinach mixture. Toss gently to coat. Makes 6 servings.

Marinated Vegetables

This make-ahead salad saves you precious minutes just before your guests arrive. (Pictured on the cover.)

1 **16-ounce package loose-pack frozen mixed broccoli, cauliflower, and carrots**

1 **small onion, thinly sliced and separated into rings**

½ **cup Italian salad dressing**

In a medium saucepan cook frozen mixed broccoli, cauliflower, and carrots in a small amount of boiling salted water about 5 minutes or till crisp-tender. Drain well.

Transfer vegetables to a bowl. Add onion and salad dressing. Toss to coat. Cover and chill for 2 to 24 hours, stirring once or twice. To serve, drain the vegetables. Makes 6 servings.

Chuck-Wagon Bean Salad

You can make this sweet-sour pasta-and-bean salad several hours before dinner to save on last-minute meal preparation.

1 cup wagon wheel *or* elbow macaroni

1 15-ounce can three-bean salad

⅓ cup mayonnaise *or* salad dressing

Lettuce leaves

■ Cook the wagon wheel or elbow macaroni according to package directions. Drain. Rinse with cold water. Drain again.

■ Drain three-bean salad, reserving *1 tablespoon* of the liquid.

■ In a medium mixing bowl combine macaroni and drained bean salad. Stir together reserved liquid and mayonnaise or salad dressing. Add to macaroni mixture. Toss to coat. Cover and chill several hours. Serve in a lettuce-lined bowl. Serves 4.

Go-Ahead on Greens

To save a last-minute step, wash your salad greens ahead of time. Remove the core from head lettuce or separate the leaves of leafy lettuce. Thoroughly rinse the greens in cold water. Drain. Pat with a clean kitchen towel or paper towels to remove water that clings to the leaves. Place the greens in a sealed plastic bag. Store 3 to 4 days in the refrigerator.

Mayo-Parmesan Bread

Surprise! No butter or margarine. Stir the Parmesan cheese right into the mayonnaise for a zippy topper.

¼ **cup grated Parmesan cheese**

¼ **cup mayonnaise *or* salad dressing**

1 **tablespoon snipped chives *or* parsley (optional)**

4 *or* **5 slices French *or* Italian bread (cut ½ inch thick)**

■ In a small mixing bowl combine Parmesan cheese and mayonnaise or salad dressing. Stir in snipped chives or parsley, if desired. Set aside.

■ Place French or Italian bread slices on the rack of an unheated broiler pan. Broil 3 to 4 inches from heat about 1 minute or till toasted.

■ Turn bread over. Spread some of the mayonnaise mixture on the untoasted side of each slice of bread. Broil, mayonnaise side up, 3 to 4 inches from heat for 2 to 3 minutes or till light brown. Makes 4 or 5 servings.

Caramel-Pecan Pinwheels

Refrigerated breadsticks come in the pinwheel shapes needed for these tasty rolls.

⅓ **cup caramel ice cream topping**

2 **tablespoons butter *or* margarine, melted**

⅓ **cup pecan halves**

1 **package (8) refrigerated breadsticks**

In a 9x1½-inch round baking pan stir together caramel ice cream topping and melted butter or margarine. Arrange pecan halves over caramel mixture.

Separate, but *do not uncoil,* refrigerated breadsticks. Arrange the dough coils atop caramel mixture. Bake in a 350° oven for 20 to 25 minutes or till golden. Let stand for 2 to 3 minutes. Loosen sides and invert rolls onto a serving platter. Serve warm. Makes 8 servings.

Apricot Pull-Aparts

Frozen bread dough starts this fancy fruit-filled loaf.

1 16-ounce loaf frozen
 white bread
 dough, thawed

1 12-ounce can
 apricot *or* prune
 cake and pastry
 filling

3 tablespoons butter
 or margarine

⅓ cup sugar

Cut bread dough in half lengthwise. Then cut each half crosswise into 8 pieces (16 pieces total). Flatten pieces of dough with fingers, stretching slightly to form 4-inch circles. Spoon about *1 tablespoon* of fruit filling in the center of *each* circle. Bring edges of dough together. Pinch to seal.

In a small saucepan melt the butter or margarine. Dip filled rolls in melted butter or margarine, then in sugar. Place, seam side down, in 2 layers in a greased 9x5x3-inch loaf pan. Cover and let rise in a warm place till almost double (about 1 hour).

Bake in a 350° oven for 35 to 40 minutes or till golden brown, covering with foil the last 10 minutes of baking. Remove from pan. Serve warm. Makes 1 loaf (8 servings).

Easy Oatmeal Muffins

A package of instant oatmeal provides apples and cinnamon.

1 egg

⅔ cup packaged
   biscuit mix

1 envelope instant
   oatmeal with
   apples and
   cinnamon

½ cup milk

In a medium mixing bowl beat egg slightly with a fork. Add biscuit mix, oatmeal, and milk. Mix till combined. Grease 6 muffin cups. Fill each cup ⅔ full with batter. Bake in a 375° oven 18 to 20 minutes or till golden. Serve warm. Makes 6.

Bistro Bagel

1 bagel, split

1 tablespoon butter
or margarine,
softened

¼ teaspoon finely
shredded
orange peel

Ground cinnamon

Toast bagel under the broiler. Meanwhile, stir together butter or margarine and orange peel. Spread each bagel half with butter mixture. Sprinkle each with cinnamon. Return to broiler. Broil till just bubbly. Makes 1 serving.

Gorp 'n' Spice Cupcakes

1 package 1-layer-size spice cake mix

⅓ cup mixed dried fruit bits

⅓ cup miniature semisweet chocolate pieces

¼ cup chopped pecans

▪ Line muffin cups with paper bake cups. Set aside. Prepare cake mix according to the package directions, *except* use only *⅓ cup* water. Stir in fruit bits.

▪ Fill each muffin cup ⅔ full. Sprinkle the chocolate pieces and chopped pecans over the tops. Bake in a 350° oven about 20 minutes or till a wooden toothpick inserted in the center comes out clean. Makes 12 cupcakes.

Sunshine Sauced Cake

This company-special dessert is a cinch to make with frozen pound cake and ready-made pudding. (Pictured on the cover.)

2 **oranges**

1 **4½-ounce container vanilla pudding**

1 **tablespoon orange liqueur**

1 **frozen loaf pound cake (10¾ ounces), thawed**

■ Finely shred enough peel from oranges to make *1 tablespoon.* Set aside. Remove and discard the remaining peel. Section oranges. Set aside.

■ In a small mixing bowl stir together vanilla pudding and orange liqueur. Cut the pound cake into 12 slices. Place *two* slices on *each* of 6 individual dessert plates. Top *each* serving with some orange sections and pudding-liqueur mixture. Sprinkle with reserved orange peel. Makes 6 servings.

Black Forest Brownies

We took a classic recipe and transformed it into a super simple yet impressive dessert.

1 roll refrigerated brownie cookie dough

1 21-ounce can cherry pie filling

¼ cup sliced almonds

▓ Divide cookie dough in half. Spread over the bottoms of 2 greased 8x1½-inch round baking pans. Bake in a 350° oven about 30 minutes or till edges are firm. Cool in pans on wire racks for 10 minutes. Remove from pans. Cool well.

▓ Place *one* brownie layer on a serving plate. Reserve *½ cup* pie filling. Spoon remaining pie filling over brownie layer. Place the second brownie layer on top of filling. Top with reserved pie filling. Sprinkle with almonds. Makes 10 to 12 servings.

Frosted Bites

For a chocolate-mint version, thin the chocolate frosting with white crème de menthe instead of water.

½ of a 17¼-ounce package frozen puff pastry (1 sheet)

½ cup canned chocolate frosting

¼ cup finely chopped pistachio nuts *or* pecans

■ Thaw pastry for 20 minutes at room temperature or overnight in the refrigerator. Unfold pastry. Cut on the 3 fold lines. Then cut each piece crosswise into 7 rectangles (21 total).

■ Arrange pastry rectangles on an ungreased baking sheet. Prick several times with a fork. Bake in a 425° oven for 15 to 20 minutes or till light brown. Transfer to a wire rack.

■ Stir 3 to 4 teaspoons *water* into chocolate frosting. Spoon frosting over tops of warm pastries. Immediately sprinkle with chopped nuts. Cool thoroughly. Makes 21 pastries.

Daiquiri Dessert

This creamy strawberry dessert requires just two easy steps—blend and fold. Then, spoon into dishes and serve.

1 10-ounce package frozen strawberries, broken up

¼ cup light rum

2 tablespoons lemon juice

1 8-ounce container frozen whipped dessert topping, thawed

▇ In a blender container or food processor bowl combine strawberries, light rum, and lemon juice. Cover and blend or process till thoroughly mixed.

▇ Transfer strawberry mixture to a medium mixing bowl. Fold in dessert topping. Spoon into 8 chilled sherbet dishes or stemmed glasses. Garnish with fresh strawberries, if desired. Serve immediately. Makes 8 servings.

Sherry Tortoni

To serve these make-ahead desserts, just take them from the freezer and top with toasted sliced almonds.

2	cups marshmallows
¼	cup cream sherry
1	cup whipping cream
2	tablespoons chopped almonds, toasted

■ In a saucepan combine marshmallows and sherry. Cook over low heat till marshmallows melt, stirring occasionally. Remove from heat. Cool for 10 minutes, stirring frequently.

■ In a chilled large mixer bowl beat whipping cream till soft peaks form. Fold marshmallow mixture into whipped cream. Fold in chopped almonds. Spoon into 6 muffin cups lined with paper bake cups. Cover and freeze 4 hours or till firm.

■ To store in the freezer, remove tortoni from muffin cups and place in moisture- and vaporproof containers in the freezer. Before serving, top with additional toasted sliced almonds, if desired. Makes 6 servings.

Microwave directions

■ In a 1-quart microwave-safe casserole combine marshmallows and sherry. Micro-cook, uncovered, on 100% power (high) for 1 to 2 minutes or till marshmallows melt, stirring once. Continue as directed above.

Dandy Candy Ice Cream

You'll find the candy-coated chocolate pieces easy to chop if you use your blender or food processor.

1 cup candy-coated milk chocolate pieces, chopped

½ of a 14-ounce can (scant ⅔ cup) *sweetened condensed* milk

2 cups whipping cream

■ In a medium mixing bowl combine candy-coated milk chocolate pieces and sweetened condensed milk. Set aside.

■ In a large mixer bowl beat the whipping cream with an electric mixer on medium speed till soft peaks form. Fold candy mixture into whipped cream. Transfer to a 9x9x2-inch pan. Cover tightly with moisture- and vaporproof wrap. Freeze 6 hours or till firm.

■ To serve, scoop ice cream into dessert dishes. Sprinkle with additional chopped candy-coated milk chocolate pieces, if desired. Makes about 1 quart (8 servings).

Mucho Mocha Mousse

You can serve this 10-minute dessert right away or make it a few hours ahead and chill it for serving later.

1½ cups milk

2 teaspoons instant coffee crystals

1 4-serving-size package *instant* chocolate pudding mix

1 1¼-ounce envelope whipped dessert topping mix

■ In a large mixer bowl combine milk and coffee crystals. Let stand 5 minutes to dissolve crystals.

■ Stir in pudding mix and dessert topping mix. Beat with an electric mixer on low speed about 30 seconds or till moistened. Beat on high speed about 4 minutes more or till fluffy. Spoon into 6 individual dessert dishes. Serve immediately or chill till serving time. Makes 6 servings.

Sure-Bet Surprise Cups

Choose any sherbet flavor—lime, raspberry, orange, or pineapple.

¼ **cup semisweet chocolate pieces**

2 **1-inch white truffles**

½ **cup sherbet**

2 **tablespoons crème de cacao**

In a small heavy saucepan cook and stir chocolate pieces over low heat till melted. Place 1 paper bake cup in each of 2 muffin or custard cups. Spoon *half* of the melted chocolate into *each*. Using a narrow metal spatula, spread chocolate over the bottoms and up sides of paper cups. Chill till firm.

Just before serving, carefully peel off paper bake cups. Place *one* white truffle in *each* chocolate cup. Using a tablespoon, scoop the sherbet into thin petals. Arrange sherbet over and around the truffles in chocolate cups. Pour *1 tablespoon* crème de cacao over sherbet in *each* cup. Makes 2 servings.

Microwave Directions

In a 1-cup glass measure micro-cook the chocolate pieces, uncovered, on 100% power (high) about 1 minute or till soft enough to stir smooth. Continue as directed above.

72

Mississippi Mud Sauce

*Serve this peanut butter and chocolate sauce over ice cream
or sliced pound cake for a super-quick dessert.*

¾ **cup sugar**

⅓ **cup unsweetened
cocoa powder**

1 **5-ounce can (⅔
cup) evaporated
milk**

¼ **cup chunky peanut
butter**

■ In a small saucepan stir together the sugar and cocoa powder.
Stir in evaporated milk. Cook and stir over medium-high
heat till mixture is boiling. Remove from heat. Stir in peanut
butter till smooth. Serve warm over ice cream or sliced pound
cake. Makes 1½ cups sauce.

 Microwave Directions

■ In a small microwave-safe mixing bowl stir together the sugar
and cocoa powder. Stir in the evaporated milk. Micro-cook,
uncovered, on 100% power (high) for 2 to 3 minutes or till
mixture is boiling, stirring once. Stir in chunky peanut butter
till smooth. Serve as directed above.

73

Merrymakers' Mushrooms

For a large party, double the recipe and stagger the baking so your guests have stuffed mushrooms hot from the oven.

16 to 20 large fresh mushrooms

1 small zucchini, shredded (¾ cup)

2 tablespoons sliced green onion

⅓ cup grated Parmesan cheese

■ Remove the stems from the mushrooms. Set the mushroom caps aside. Chop the stems.

■ In a medium saucepan combine mushroom stems, zucchini, green onion, and 1 tablespoon *water*. Cook and stir over medium heat till vegetables are tender. Drain. Stir Parmesan cheese into vegetable mixture.

■ Divide vegetable mixture among the mushroom caps. Place stuffed mushrooms in a 13x9x2-inch baking dish. Bake in a 375° oven for 8 to 10 minutes or till mushroom caps are tender. Serve warm. Makes 16 to 20 appetizers.

Vegetable Pita Pockets

Try any creamy salad dressing you have on hand to add zip to these cheese- and vegetable-filled pita wedges.

8 6-inch white *or* whole wheat pita bread rounds

½ cup creamy bacon salad dressing

32 pieces cooked broccoli flowerets, baby carrots, pea pods, asparagus cuts, *and/or* cauliflower flowerets

4 slices American cheese

▪ Cut pita bread rounds into quarters. Spread the inside of each quarter with creamy bacon salad dressing. Place 1 vegetable piece in each pita quarter.

▪ Cut each cheese slice into 4 strips. Halve each strip crosswise. Place 1 cheese piece in each pita quarter. Secure bundles with wooden toothpicks, if necessary. Place on a baking sheet.

▪ Bake in a 375° oven about 5 minutes or till cheese starts to melt. Serve immediately. Makes 32 appetizers.

Pizza Bubble Bread

*For this saucy pizza snack, start with a crust made from
refrigerated biscuits.*

Cornmeal

**1 package (10)
    refrigerated
    biscuits**

**½ cup spaghetti *or*
    pizza sauce**

**1 cup shredded
    mozzarella cheese
    (4 ounces)**

■ Sprinkle a greased 12-inch pizza pan with cornmeal. Separate
biscuits. Snip each biscuit into 4 pieces. Place in a medium
mixing bowl. Add spaghetti or pizza sauce. Toss to coat.

■ Arrange biscuit dough pieces in an 8-inch circle in the pizza
pan. Sprinkle with the mozzarella cheese.

■ Bake in a 400° oven about 15 minutes or till golden. Makes
10 to 12 appetizer servings.

Piquant Chutney Dip

Make this sweet-sour dip with assorted dippers for drop-in guests.

1 **9-ounce jar chutney**

1 **tablespoon vinegar**

Cooked shrimp *or*
**cooked frozen
breaded small
chunk-shape
chicken patties**

Green pepper strips

■ Chop or snip any large pieces in the chutney. In a small saucepan combine chutney and vinegar. Cook and stir till heated through. If necessary, add enough *water* to make the mixture of dipping consistency.

■ Transfer dip to a serving dish. Place on a platter. Arrange shrimp or chicken and green pepper strips around dip for dippers. Makes about ⅔ cup dip.

Microwave Directions

■ In a 2-cup glass measure combine chutney and vinegar. Micro-cook, uncovered, on 100% power (high) for 1 to 2 minutes or till heated through. Serve as directed above.

Pepper-Cheese Balls

For variety, roll some in parsley and some in peanuts.

1 **cup shredded
   cheddar cheese
   (4 ounces)**

1 **3-ounce package
   cream cheese
   with chives**

1 **4-ounce can
   diced green chili
   peppers, drained**

**Finely chopped
   peanuts** *or*
   snipped parsley

■ Bring cheddar cheese and cream cheese to room temperature. In a medium mixing bowl mix together cheddar cheese, cream cheese, and green chili peppers till well blended.

■ Shape the cheese mixture into 18 bite-size balls. Roll cheese balls in peanuts or parsley. Chill 3 hours or till serving time. Makes 18 appetizers.

Cashews and Raisins

Add a container of this snack mix to a brown-bag lunch.

1½ cups raw cashews

1 tablespoon
    butter *or*
    margarine

¾ teaspoon pumpkin
    pie *or* apple pie
    spice

¾ cup raisins

■ In a medium skillet combine cashews and butter or margarine. Cook over medium heat, stirring constantly, for 5 minutes.

■ Stir in pumpkin pie or apple pie spice. Cook and stir about 3 minutes more or till the cashews are toasted. Add raisins and toss to coat. Spread mixture on a baking sheet or on foil to cool. Makes 10 servings (2½ cups).

 Microwave Directions

■ In a 1½-quart microwave-safe casserole place butter or margarine. Micro-cook, uncovered, on 100% power (high) for 45 to 60 seconds or till melted. Add cashews, stirring well to coat. Cook, uncovered, on high for 3 minutes, stirring once.

■ Add pumpkin pie or apple pie spice. Stir well to coat cashews. Cook, uncovered, on high for 3½ to 4½ minutes or till cashews are toasted, stirring every minute. Add raisins and toss to coat. Spread on baking sheet or foil to cool.

Index

If you like to cook but don't have the time, turn to BETTER HOMES AND GARDENS® *20 Minutes to Dinner* and *On-the-Go Cook Book.* In these books you'll find lots of quick and easy recipes for busy people.

Have BETTER HOMES AND GARDENS® magazine delivered to your door. For information, write to:
MR. ROBERT AUSTIN
P.O. BOX 4536
DES MOINES, IA 50336